Sydney Evans

Salisbury Cathedral

A Reflective Guide

Michael Russell

Text © Sydney Evans 1985

First published in Great Britain 1985
by Michael Russell (Publishing) Ltd
The Chantry, Wilton, Salisbury, Wiltshire

Typeset in Sabon by The Spartan Press Ltd,
Lymington, Hampshire
Printed in Great Britain by The Acorn Press,
Bournemouth, Dorset
from plates supplied by Aero Offset
(Bournemouth) Ltd

Designed by Humphrey Stone

Acknowledgements

Nobody who has lived with a medieval cathedral for a mere seven years could venture to write about its complex and fascinating history and contemporary life had he not been able to peruse scholarly studies by medievalists who had searched the Chapter Act Books and other archives, together with published appreciations of the architecture by architects and art historians. Essentially this book is a personal response to Salisbury Cathedral by an individual who has been privileged for a few years to be a guardian of its unique inheritance and, with his colleagues, to be responsible for its present maintenance and mission.

What I have to offer is a selection of observations and reflections for readers who have only a few hours in which to assimilate its story and its genius.

The colour photographs which illuminate this reflective guide were taken by Mr Mark Fiennes, as were those in monochrome on pp. 11, 12, 17, 24, 29, 37, 41, 44, 50, 54 and 58. Other photographs were taken by Mr Roy Spring, our devoted and experienced Clerk of the Works and director of our gifted team of craftsmen. Miss Christine Wevill contributed three and the details from the *Prisoners of Conscience* window are the work of Miss Sonia Halliday and Miss Laura Lushington, whose colour photographs adorn my earlier booklet telling the story of this window. The Ministry of Defence supplied the photograph on page 8.

Mr Alan Rome, our Cathedral Architect, generously made time to read the script and make valuable criticisms and suggestions. Mr Richard Seal, Organist and Choirmaster – for seventeen years the continuing inspiration of the choral offering of the choir, our daily 'heaven upon earth' – has also kindly read what I have written all too briefly about this vibrant heart of the cathedral's continuing spirituality. To Miss Suzanne Eward, Cathedral Librarian and Keeper of the Muniments, I am especially grateful, for her expert help in directing my attention to selected archives and for her close scrutiny of my text. The patience of my secretary, Miss Diane Fray, who typed and retyped the frequently altered pages of manuscript, alone enabled a coherent story to emerge. That I was sufficiently encouraged to make the attempt at all was largely due to my old friend Mr William Saumarez Smith, and to my new friend and publisher, Mr Michael Russell.

I dedicate what is here produced with great joy to that considerable company of men and women who, for love of God, serve with glad hearts and willing hands this glory that is the Cathedral of the Blessed Virgin Mary at Salisbury.

Ascension Day 1985   SYDNEY EVANS

1 *The Builders*

Suppose yourself to be living in Britain in the year 1066. It was a Britain with a population unimaginably smaller than its present size: the Domesday count for England alone in 1086 gave the number as one and a half million. Britain in 1066 was a Britain with no great cities, abbeys or cathedrals, a Britain of small monastic houses and schools, of country churches made of wattle and wood as well as of stone. Christian beliefs and practices were widely diffused, but in a distinctively British version of Christianity stemming from the missionaries led by Augustine and his monks from Europe and Rome, centred on Canterbury, and those who came from Brittany via Ireland and Iona, inspired by leaders like Columba, Aidan, Cuthbert, Wilfred, Bede and Chad. These were not the first Christians to reach these islands, but little is known about those who came when Britain was a northern outpost of the Roman Empire. The first British martyr for Christ, St Alban, is thought to have been a Roman soldier but the coming of the Normans left an even deeper imprint than the coming of Julius Caesar and his legions. We are apt to forget, too, the continuing interchange of people and ideas between Britain and Europe before the Norman Conquest and more strongly afterwards. In 781 Alcuin, the schoolmaster from York, was invited by Charlemagne to advise him in educational and ecclesiastical matters, becoming eventually Abbot of Tours where he founded an important school and library. Most of the leading churchmen who built the 'norman' and later the 'gothic' cathedrals were of Continental origin.

What the Norman Conquest was all about can be seen at a glance in two places to this day. Durham with its Norman castle and cathedral high on the acropolis above the encircling River Wear ('half church of God, half castle 'gainst the Scot') clearly demonstrates the two authorities of crown and mitre. So, too, on a smaller scale does the ruined royal castle at Old Sarum, two miles to the north of modern Salisbury. Within the enclosure of what began its human occupation as a fortified Iron Age

OPPOSITE: *The nave, looking west.*

An aerial view of Old Sarum, showing the excavated outline of the old cathedral.

town, the Normans built castle and cathedral with the bishop's house within the fortress. Church and State marched together to overawe the Saxon inhabitants with the dual authority of king and pope.

Already before the coming of the Normans, as the influence of the Gospel and the church-community of faith expanded and more of the native British were baptised, the area over which a bishop could effectively preside was found to be too large. The organisation of the Church into smaller dioceses was in the main the work of an Archbishop of Canterbury (Theodore of Tarsus, 668–85) who came from the Greek Church of the eastern Mediterranean. Ancient Wessex extended from Surrey to Cornwall and was divided into two bishoprics, Winchester and Sherborne. By the beginning of the tenth century it had become clear that so vast a tract of country was beyond the capacity of two bishops. A new plan based on division by shires assigned Wiltshire and Berkshire to the new see of Ramsbury, Dorset to Sherborne, Devon and Cornwall to Crediton, and Somerset to Wells. The diocese of Salisbury was formed in 1058 by a union of the earlier dioceses of Ramsbury and Sherborne. But it was not until 1075 that Bishop Herman moved his see from Ramsbury to Old Sarum, embracing within his jurisdiction the counties of Berkshire,

Wiltshire and Dorset. Nothing remains of the cathedral that he began and which his successor, Osmund, finished, except the excavated outline of the walls indicating periods of rebuilding and extension. More lasting than the building was Osmund's constitution for the governing of the cathedral and the ordering of its life and worship. To understand what the cathedral at Old Sarum was designed to be and to do we must first note that it was not a monastery. The clergy who served it were not monks but celibate priests called canons, living in their own houses but under rule.

Europe had for many centuries become familiar with that form of Christian community that developed from the experiences of the Desert Fathers in Egypt at the critical period when the Roman Empire was breaking up. Men like Anthony, Pachomius, Cassian, Benedict and Basil gave to the broken world of Europe, east and west, not only a fresh vision but institutions in which this vision was given form and content and a way of life which preserved the great inheritance from the classical and Hebrew past in a Christian formation. The wildness of the northern invaders was tamed and what emerged was the medieval achievement and synthesis: an achievement which found literary expression in Dante's *Divine Comedy*, architectural expression in the sculptures and stained glass of the cathedral at Chartres, and continuing social expression in the monastic communities based on the Rule of St Benedict. The pattern of worship in the cathedrals drew deeply on the liturgical experience and traditions of the Benedictine monasteries.

What, then, was it that gave rise to the secular organisation of the cathedrals? Jean Gimpel in *The Cathedral Builders* offers an explanation. Faced with the task of ministering word and sacraments to the scattered towns and villages of his diocese, the early medieval bishop would have gathered around him a group of priests to help him to administer the diocese and to celebrate the eucharist in the parishes. At first these priests were required to lead a community life, sleeping in dormitories, eating in refectories and joining together in the daily offices of prayer – more or less on the monastic pattern. In the following century it would seem that the vows of chastity and obedience were still required of the canons, but the vow of poverty fell into abeyance, thereby opening the way to the system which Osmund set out to regulate at Old Sarum.

The building and maintenance of a medieval cathedral required continuity. The chapter had this responsibility. The word 'chapter' calls for explanation. The word in its ecclesiastical use means a meeting of the canons of a cathedral church at which a chapter of scripture would be read. The word by extension also designates the persons who meet, and so becomes the name of the place where they meet; hence Chapter House. Gradually the chapter acquired privileges and property independent of the bishop, who was often absent on the king's business. It was the chapter who directed the building of the cathedral and its maintenance. The canons had their own private income from the prebends to which they were appointed and from time to time they taxed themselves to sustain the work of the building. But the chapter also built up their common fund. Inevitably chapters with a dean at their head became less and less dependent on the bishop. Arguments, if not quarrels, about rights and privileges were not infrequent. But it was the chapter who were in charge of the building and responsible for raising the money needed and for administering the accumulated funds. The bishop might or might not himself contribute to the raising of money for the building fund and the maintenance of the fabric. Many did and generously.

When Osmund became bishop at Old Sarum in 1078 he worked out a set of regulations to enable the chapter to fulfil their duties with the minimum of friction or negligence. He appointed four 'principal persons' whose stalls were to be placed at the four corners of the choir. The precentor was given charge of music and of arrangements for worship; the chancellor was made responsible for education; the treasurer was given charge of fabric and furnishings; and the dean was to be the coordinator of it all and to preside at chapter meetings, which, when all the canons were present, could number fifty-two persons. This way of ordering the management of a cathedral was adopted in due course by most of the British medieval cathedrals that were not staffed by monks, and it continues to this day – a notable tribute to the wise perceptions of its originator.

Episcopal estates in Dorset, Wiltshire and Berkshire became sources of endowment for the cathedral; other property was given for the souls of King William, Queen Maud, their son William II, and for Bishop Osmund by charter of 1091. The names of the first deans suggest that they were Normans; but Anglo-Saxon traditions of Christianity do not seem to have been forgotten. Osmund took trouble to procure for his cathedral a relic of St Aldhelm, his predecessor as Bishop of Sherborne three hundred years before. Osmund himself was not declared saint until 1456. Records show that the original property of the chapter had more than doubled in the twelfth and thirteenth centuries by gifts from kings, lay magnates, bishops and other clergy and laity. Henry I was a generous benefactor. By such

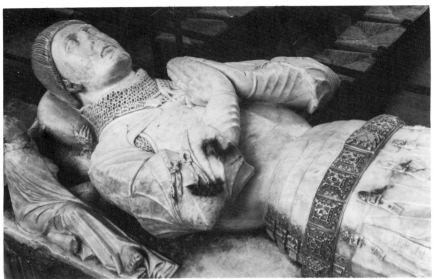

Tomb of Sir John Cheyney (d. 1509), standard-bearer of Henry of Richmond, later Henry VII, at the Battle of Bosworth.

bequests the chapter became a rich and privileged corporation. During the last fifty years at Old Sarum efforts were made to direct more of the endowments to the common fund, partly in order to make residence financially more attractive to those canons who found living in their prebendal properties more to their liking.

Before taking leave of Old Sarum for New we must make mention of John of Salisbury, a boy from Bishop Osmund's grammar school who, after further education in Paris and Chartres, became confidential secretary first to Archbishop Theobald and then to Archbishop Thomas à Becket. A collection of his official and personal letters, 325 in all, has survived, giving an invaluable insight into ecclesiastical affairs of the time. John was in France during the period of the Archbishop's exile, preceded his return to Canterbury and was present in the cathedral when Becket was murdered. Subsequently John became Bishop of Chartres until his death in 1180.

Once the authority of the Normans over the Saxon population had been established, it must have become more and more irksome for the canons to be confined within a cathedral close that was itself confined within a hill fortress under military management. There was nothing new

about the inconveniences listed by the dean and chapter in their letter to Pope Honorius III in 1217 requesting his consent to their wish to build afresh two miles to the south in the valley of the Avon. Probably friction between garrison and cathedral had reached boiling point; but there could well have been another powerful influence at work. Remembering the continuing movement of individuals to and from the Continent, it is not unreasonable to suppose that the chapter at Old Sarum were well aware of what was happening in France and by contrast felt their own frustrations more acutely. Between 1130 and 1284 the great gothic cathedrals of the north of France were created. Surely men like Richard Poore, dean and later bishop, and Elias of Dereham, the master builder, were caught by this enthusiasm; just as there must be a connection between Henry III's interest in the new cathedral at Salisbury and his decision to rebuild Westminster Abbey. Nobody who knows the interior of both Westminster and Salisbury can fail to notice the architectural similarities.

In the strict sense, the builders of the cathedrals were the deans and chapters. At Salisbury, if the initial inspiration and drive came from Richard Poore (in 1228 he was translated to the see of Durham), there seems general agreement that the man placed in charge of the actual building enterprise was Elias of Dereham and that the master mason was Nicholas of Ely.

But there could be no building without money and materials. The patronage of Henry III and his gifts of money and timber influenced other magnates to open their coffers, but it would seem that, despite his name, Bishop Poore was a rich man, and it was he in all probability who owned and gave the land on which the cathedral, the bishop's palace and the canons' houses were to be built. At the beginning of 1219 it was agreed that all canons and vicars should contribute a fixed portion from their prebends and stipends to the fabric for seven years. Seven dignitaries and canons travelled the country raising money, going as far as Scotland and Ireland. Leland tells us that one of the benefactors, Lady Alicia Bruere, contributed marble and stone from Purbeck for twelve years.

Another source of finance for building cathedrals was a consequence of the decline in the popularity of going on pilgrimage or crusade to the Holy Land. The giving of indulgences to those who made those expeditions was

OPPOSITE: *Statues at the north corner of the west front. The figure on the left is Bishop Poore holding a model of the cathedral.*

no longer required, so the idea developed of granting indulgences to people who gave money towards the building of cathedrals. We have in the cathedral archives the original of an indult of Edmund, Archbishop of Canterbury (1234–40) granting a relaxation of forty days of penance to contributors to the fabric of Salisbury Cathedral. Edmund had been treasurer of Salisbury at the time of the move from Old Sarum. The document retells the reasons why the first cathedral had been abandoned and a new building begun, and ends:

We, being fully assured of the mercy of Jesus Christ and the merits of the blessed and glorious Virgin Mary, grant remission from forty days of their required penance to all who by gift or transfer contribute from the goods that God has given them towards the building of the aforesaid church and we declare them to be sharers in the aforesaid church and we declare them to be sharers in the benefits of all the prayers that are offered in the holy church of Canterbury.

Indulgence granted by Edmund of Abingdon, Archbishop of Canterbury c. 1235, remitting forty days' penance to those who contributed to the building.

The foundation stone was laid on 28 April 1220 and the essential work took thirty years. By 1225 the east end had reached the stage where three altars could be consecrated at an impressive ceremony at which Archbishop Stephen Langton preached. The whole church was consecrated in 1258 and the roofing with lead was finished by 1266. North-west of the nave a great belfry was built of which the foundations can still be traced on the grass after a dry summer. The Cloisters and Chapter House followed between 1263 and 1280.

Surprisingly and tantalisingly there is no document surviving to tell us when the work on the tower and spire was begun or completed. Conjectures as to the date when the stumpy lantern tower at the crossing was raised to the present tower and spire have never resulted in a confident conclusion. It would be natural to think that there was no break in the work and that the tower building followed on from the completion of the Cloisters and Chapter House. Even without binoculars the discerning eye will remark a difference in style. The faces of the tower are more elaborately decorated; the dogtooth ornamentation has been changed into the ball-flower. Such a development in style could well result from a new company of stonecutters and a new master mason bringing new ideas from elsewhere. Pevsner states that 'the contract for this work dates from 1334'. He quotes no evidence. Probably he is referring to an agreement dated 6 June 1335 drawn up between Richard of Farley and the dean and chapter. But this agreement outlines only general conditions and not any specific work. It is hard to believe that a contract involving a commission for a project as daunting as the building of tower and spire could have been drafted without a clear statement to that effect. A start as late as 1334 would have run into the catastrophic disaster of the Black Death which hit Europe in 1347 and reached Salisbury in the late summer of 1348. Estimates suggest that between a third and a half of the population of the British Isles died from this pestilence. Would it have been possible for such a major construction to have been completed without many years of inactivity had it been started as late as 1334?

An extract from a patent of the first year of Henry VI (1423) reads: 'That the stone tower standing in the middle of Salisbury Cathedral is become ruinous and the Dean and Chapter are thereby empowered to appropriate £50 annually for its repair.' Some have argued that this refers to repair to the original lantern and was made the occasion for the adding of the present tower and spire. We note that the strainer arches between the main transepts at the central crossing under the tower were inserted at the beginning of the fifteenth century to withstand the side thrust of the tower. When one looks at the degree of inclination of pillars in choir and transepts, the first half of the fifteenth century may seem a late date for the insertion of the strainer arches if the tower and spire had been completed by the end of the third decade of the fourteenth. The inverted bracing arches, however, which strengthened the high choir arches of the east transepts were added, it would appear, at a much earlier date. In the absence of new evidence it seems best to follow Gleeson White writing in 1901, and Roy Spring, clerk of the works, writing in 1982 after fifteen years of observation of the entire cathedral structure, and to prefer a continuous building programme with the spire completed before the Black Death. Roy Spring writes:

Support for this can be gained by studying the list of deans and bishops in *Fasti Ecclesiae Sarisburiensis*. Those from 1258–1297 mostly took an interest in the fabric and are entered in its calendar of benefactors. Three of these deans also became bishops of Salisbury, therefore retaining their interest in the building work. From 1297–1379 the deans are foreign, two being Cardinal priests, three being relatives of Pope Clement V. Their duties elsewhere would have left them little time for taking more than a passing interest in Salisbury . . . When looked at from a practical point of view it is logical to keep work going continuously; having gathered together a group of craftsmen, it is much easier to maintain enthusiasm if a long programme of work can be seen ahead.

Whatever the truth of the matter of date, the work was achieved. To be up in the tower today when a strong wind is roaring round outside is to be given a very deep respect for the scaffolders, masons and carpenters who worked at this height in all weathers.

Too little thought has been given to the craftsmen who did the physical work of building the cathedrals of France and Britain. You realise that behind the unity of style and the soaring audacious beauty of its exterior form are the designers, the master masons, the woodworkers and stonecutters, the foresters who cut down the trees and the quarrymen who extracted the stone and marble from Chilmark and Purbeck. Something of the order of 120,000 tons of stone had to be cut from the quarries at Chilmark for the building of Salisbury Cathedral, carted the distance, cut to shape and hauled to the height at which building was being done.

OPPOSITE: *Strainer arches, seen from the north east (choir) transept.*

The cathedral from the north east: a Matterhorn of dressed and sculptured stone.

2 The Exterior

The most breathtaking introduction to Salisbury Cathedral is to enter the Close by way of St Ann's Gate. Illuminated at night, the cathedral is like a splendid ship, her 'white sails crowding', moving majestically over the dark-green waters of the Close. Nor is this mere fantasy. Built on virgin water-meadows between the years 1220 and 1258 (the tower, spire and cloisters were added later) the water-table to this day is only five feet below ground level. The entire soaring, heavenward pointing hull and superstructure is upheld on a bed of gravel. The stone foundations of the four pillars that carry the weight of tower and spire are only four feet into the ground.

So the question is raised: was the tower and spire originally 'seen' in the artist's vision? If 'seen and intended', then why were foundations not laid that would be more adequate to their anticipated load? But this structural question needs to be balanced with an artistic question. 'Could an artist have imagined the effect on the eye of the retro-choir, high choir, nave and transepts as we see them today and not have felt that what he envisaged even at that stage *demanded* completion in central tower and spire?'

For us everything takes our eyes up from ground base to the apex of the spire – the angles of the gable ends, the slope of the lead roofs, the pinnacles and finials, the upward-pointing lancet windows – everything *demands* the culmination we marvel at. Yet the fact remains that the foundations were not such as any responsible master mason could have conscientiously laid had he anticipated the weight the pillars were ultimately destined to carry. All the more audacious then, if not intended from the start, was the decision to obey the *demand* of the finished nave, choir and transepts for central tower and spire in the knowledge that the foundations had not been adequately prepared. What a lost treasure it is that those who built did not leave any written account of what was in their mind and heart. But the greater treasure is the spire itself standing 'straight, true and glorious against the sky'.

Observed in the clear light of a spring morning or in the sunset glow of an autumn evening, the cathedral gives the impression of serenity, perfect

Gables and pinnacles.

Metal bonds and stone buttresses.

poise and peace. In fact what we see is peace resulting from an equilibrium of tensions. One of the most interesting studies that the cathedral offers is the study of these thrusts and tensions. Even without the tower and spire, the weight of the vaults and roofs is only prevented from thrusting the nave pillars and aisle walls outwards by the counteravailing inward thrust of the exterior buttresses. The transepts also act as weight-bearing and thrust-carrying buttresses. Add tower and many tons of masonry on to the central pillars at the crossing and a vastly increased problem of weight and thrust calls for continuing vigilance from the builders. It calls, too, for a craftsmanship quick to insert interior as well as exterior additional buttresses wherever extra support is seen to be needed. Where an architect of our day would have had the mathematics of weight and thrust worked out in advance of building, and where structural engineers and quantity surveyors would have insisted on the necessary precautions, the medieval masons could only work from experiment and observation of movement anywhere in the entire building as more and more weight was added to tower and spire. Something of these emergency strengthenings can be observed outside the cathedral in the shape of flying buttresses.

But what of the stone itself? The grey stone from Chilmark, which causes some people to express disappointment with the interior of the cathedral, has its own special charm for those who are able to observe the exterior in the changing seasons. The stone is hospitable to a particular lichen which is green in wet weather but presents itself in varying shades of russet during dry summer months. To ensure this quality of strength and colour the dean and chapter have reopened one of the Chilmark quarry-mines. From this will come a supply of stone to meet the needs of masons working in years to come to replace the weather-worn decorative carving on spire, tower, west front, parapets and pinnacles, and to repair the weight-bearing structures.

Reading the interior from the outside we can see how the rectangular layout in the form of a cross of Lorraine dictates the exterior shapes. The four arms of the cross are the four transepts, two shorter ones towards the east end; two larger ones towards the west forming the main crossing beneath the tower and supporting the superstructure in position. The building is 449 feet long; the vaults are 81 feet high inside; the height of the spire is 404 feet – the tallest in England. Amiens in France, built at the same time, is as immense as Salisbury is intimate. The vault at Amiens is carried at 139 feet, but there is no cloud-piercing spire. Comparison of these two superb structures illustrates the difference of vision of the French and English builders.

The eastern end of the cathedral houses the Trinity Chapel, and it was here that Bishop Poore laid foundation stones in 1220. He laid one for the Pope, one for Archbishop Stephen Langton, one for himself. William Longespée, Earl of Sarum, and his wife, the Countess Ela, laid two more. Six years later the Earl was to be the first person to be buried in the as yet far from finished cathedral. From the fifteenth century until the eighteenth there were two chantry chapels flanking the Trinity Chapel: Beauchamp on the south and Hungerford on the north. Both these additions were removed towards the end of the eighteenth century as part of the controversial changes carried out by the architect James Wyatt on the instruction of the dean and chapter. We are familiar with stories and indeed with evidence of destructive acts carried out by the commissioners of Henry VIII and later by Cromwell's soldiers during the Civil War and Commonwealth. But far more serious destruction was ordered by authority in cathedrals and medieval churches in France and England by later architects and their masters on the strength of some theory or *idée fixe*. The impressive belfry recorded in early eighteenth-century prints standing opposite the north-west porch fell to the demolition men, no doubt because there was no money to achieve a complete restoration. But on the credit side, certain dwelling houses that had been allowed to be built on the inside of the boundaries of the north and west walks were also removed. The headstones of graves were either removed and inserted in the floor of the cathedral or were laid down on the top of the tombs and grassed over, thereby making possible the extensive grass surround and the trees.

What the exterior of the cathedral invites us to do is to observe it, to sit on a bench and look until we really begin to see what those masons did. They achieved the most unified architectural ensemble of all the English cathedrals. The chief recurrent features are the windows, often shafted with Purbeck marble outside and mostly so inside. The tall single lancet window is characteristic of the Early English gothic style. We observe that the lancets are in pairs and triplets and sometimes in clusters of five. The windows at the apex of the nave and transept gables give light to the areas above the stone vault of the interior and below the outer roof. Here is a world on its own, with great timbers and walkways for the maintenance men, for firemen in an emergency and for visitors who choose to take a tour of vault and tower. The style overall is the same. Variations are introduced by different clusters of windows in different sizes. The decorative stonework is simple and restrained. We note how the groups of five, closely placed set-offs on the buttresses about two-thirds of the way up have the effect of binding the whole building together horizontally, girdling the whole visually with a kind of belt. A similar device, no doubt to throw off rain water, is to be seen at the base of walls and buttresses; another course falls below the sill level of windows. The panelled top parapet and frieze of pointed trefoils is also simple and pleasing. If these decorative features were allowed to decay further without restoration the impoverishment of the whole would offend the eye. Two other features deserve our notice: the steep flying buttresses which steady the east wall on the north and south side of the high choir, and the more elaborate decoration of a later date that characterises the four faces of the tower, together with the cluster of pinnacles around the base of the spire. These pinnacles have been so placed that the eye passes happily from the square of the tower to the tapering octagon of the spire. It is a triumph of both engineering and artistic skill.

A different view of the exterior is gained from the south side, from the private grounds of the Salisbury Cathedral School which is now housed in

Exterior of the east end.

North wall of the Cloisters, looking west.

OPPOSITE: *Tower, spire and Chapter House from the grounds of the Cathedral School.*

the old bishop's palace, formerly lived in by bishops of Salisbury from 1220 until 1947. From this angle the contours of the cathedral are elaborated by the Cloisters and Chapter House and by the small bastion which houses the Canons' Vestry on the ground floor and above it the Song School where choristers and lay vicars meet to practise the music of the services with the choirmaster. Until 1969 this upper room, with its fine strong timber roof springing from a central wooden column and with its floor of medieval tiles, was the Muniment Room containing the cathedral archives.

Cloisters are a feature of monastic buildings, so the provision of these particularly splendid cloisters in a secular cathedral was something of a *jeu d'esprit*. They invite a quiet walk round with pauses to look up at the

The top of the single central pillar of the Chapter House and the fan vaulting.

spire from this vantage point. The Chapter House entrance is on the east side, a gracious room that invites comparison with that at Westminster and that at Wells. Around the walls of this octagonal building are the stone seats for the members of the greater chapter presided over by the dean. In these days the effective chapter consists of the dean and three residentiary canons. Non-residentiary canons are parish priests resident in the parishes of the diocese who come together only twice a year. The Chapter House has long ceased to be used for its medieval purpose and after recent restoration has become a place to display our most treasured possession, one of the only four remaining original copies of Magna Carta of 1215, together with six cases of silver plate, most of it lent to the cathedral by parochial church councils. In addition there are two cases of historical documents and rare books from the cathedral archives and library, reminding us that the cathedral is a continuing community of persons as well as a building of surpassing excellence. The slender central pillar, brilliantly renewed in the nineteenth century, spreading out like an umbrella of stone, is surrounded with many exquisite examples of fourteenth-century carving of leaf foliage, of nameless faces full of

Nineteenth-century statues by Redfern on the west front.

personality, and the encircling sculpture of episodes from the books of Genesis and Exodus. Well-preserved designs of medieval painting adorn the vaults of the entrance, and the arch through which the visitor passes into the Chapter House is decorated with delicate figures representing Virtues and Vices.

South of the Cloisters are the workshops, where, as in centuries past, the clerk of the works organises the daily tasks of woodworkers, stonemasons, glaziers and plumbers. The upkeep of the fabric of a building more than 700 years old is an ever-unfinished task.

Outside on the west side of the cathedral we pause again to take in the elaborate structure of the west front. This is a screen façade, somewhat awkwardly attached to the west end rather than growing organically out of the nave and aisles. The unsatisfactory design and layout of the west front has been analysed by Nikolaus Pevsner in the Wiltshire volume of his *Buildings of England* in what he calls 'pages of embarrassed criticism'. Most of the figures in the niches were carved in the nineteenth century by Redfern. There are eight surviving figures from the fourteenth century and these can be easily identified by extreme decay. This west front of

Salisbury does not measure up to the quality of the rest of the building and at present the stonework is in need of radical restoration. The so-called 'Baker' treatment which has brought to life the statues at Wells and Exeter has been started with encouraging results on both medieval and nineteenth-century statues at Salisbury. One of our young masons spent two years at the Wells west front restoration to learn the process. In essence the 'Baker' treatment cleans and consolidates the friable, sulphate encrusted stone by means of lime poultices and repeated sprays of lime water.

The custom of creating a gallery of sculptured figures with a theological intention on the west front of cathedrals can be studied especially well in France, and in England notably at Exeter and Wells. The west front of Wells in medieval times, when all would be brightly coloured, must in the light of the setting sun, have looked like a page of an illuminated manuscript: a sculptured *Credo*; a *Te Deum* in stone.

Thomas Hardy's midnight reflections on *A Cathedral Façade* speak of a different erosion:

> Along the sculptures of the western wall
>   I watched the moonlight creeping:
> It moved as if it hardly moved at all,
>   Inch by inch thinly peeping
> Round on the pious figures of freestone, brought
> And poised there when the Universe was wrought
> To serve its centre, Earth, in mankind's thought.
>
> The lunar look skimmed scantly toe, breast, arm,
>   Then edged on slowly, slightly,
> To shoulder, hand, face; till each austere form
>   Was blanched its whole length brightly
> Of prophet, king, queen, cardinal in state
> That dead men's tools had striven to simulate;
> And the stiff images stood irradiate.
>
> A frail moan from the martyred saints there set
>   Mid others of the erection
> Against the breeze, seemed sighings of regret
>   At the ancient faith's rejection
> Under the sure, unhasting, steady stress
> Of Reason's movement, making meaningless
> The coded creeds of old-time godliness.

But a chapter on the exterior of Salisbury Cathedral can only end with

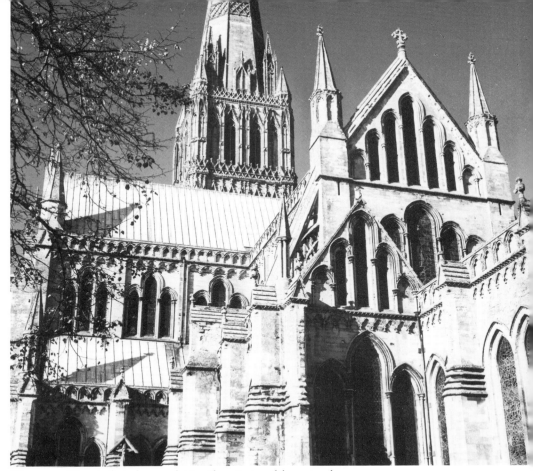

The upward thrust of windows and spire: the exterior of the east end.

praise and thanksgiving. Let that encomium be in the words of one who has written so memorably about the community of the Close. Dora Robertson in *Sarum Close*:

This is the age of Faith, and yet how short men fall of their hopes and aspirations. There is the great building which symbolises them – it rises above us like a cliff, a stupendous mass of masonry, yet every stone instinct with grace and beauty. Majestic and eternal, its spire points upwards to the unattainable ideal towards which we strive. And yet there is comfort in the thought that the men who raised this building in the past, and those who serve it now, although so petty and frail in their humanity, yet have a genius within them capable of rising to such tremendous heights. Only the saints, so few and far between, can mirror this loveliness in their lives; flaming they stand, lone torches down the ages, irradiating with their fire the intervening darkness. And yet all men have in their hearts a grain of the faith which has conceived this imperishable beauty, this Spirit made visible in stone.

3 The Interior

On entering the cathedral the first thing to do is to sit down. Indeed, if you are to appreciate the interior you will be wise on your journey to sit down at different vantage points and to survey at leisure and at rest what is around you and above. A cathedral, like any great work of art, calls for contemplation. What the artist has done needs to be assimilated by way of attentive looking. To treat a cathedral as if it were a museum, moving with a catalogue from exhibit to exhibit, from chapel to chapel, from tomb to tomb, would be to miss the meaning and the splendour of the whole by undue concentration on the parts. The architectural achievement is more deserving of contemplation than the particular antiquarian deposits of the centuries, important and interesting as they undoubtedly are in contributing to a feeling for the cathedral as the centre of a continuing community through the ages. As Philip Larkin has written:

> A serious house on serious earth it is,
> In whose blent air all our compulsions meet,
> Are recognised, and robed as destinies.
> And that much never can be obsolete,
> Since someone will forever be surprising
> A hunger in himself to be more serious,
> And gravitating with it to this ground,
> Which, he once heard, was proper to grow wise in,
> If only that so many dead lie round.

THE LESS DECEIVED (1955)

Without the builders, without the community of faith, there would be no building. Each generation adds and takes away, repairs and maintains the inheritance. And what is the inheritance if not the primary vision translated into walls and windows, pillars and arches rising to triforium and clerestory and the over-branching vaults? And all this built to provide a canopy over the acts of a worshipping community of believers, an

OPPOSITE: *Looking through the nave and choir to the Trinity Chapel and Prisoners of Conscience window at the east end.*

Sir Richard Mompesson and Katherine, his wife. The opulent seventeenth-century tomb was moved from its original place with the result that contrary to traditional custom the pair face west and not east.

organisation of space in which movement and music, word and sacrament, can be presented with dignity befitting an action which is nothing less than a celebration of the Christian understanding of the meaning and mystery of being alive and being human. A cathedral is a theatre for a kind of liturgical dance to the music of time and the hidden harmonies of God. The building itself is a drama, no less than the worship it was built to shelter and inspire.

Put more starkly, a cathedral is essentially a stone covering for a basin, a table and a chair. The *basin* is the font, where new members are initiated into the community of faith by a simple ceremony with water and words and a lighted candle. The *table* is the altar around which the initiated gather as a family for a special kind of meal with bread and wine. The accompanying words link what is being done backwards in time to that gathering of Jesus with his friends in an upper room in Jerusalem on the night in which he was betrayed by a friend and dragged to a cruel death by crucifixion. The words also link the acts and the worshippers with the life-enhancing presence of the one who was crucified but who has been experienced by the faithful over nearly twenty centuries as the animating spirit of a new way of living human life in the here and now. The *chair* is the *cathedra* of the bishop of the diocese; from this Greek word for a chair a cathedral takes its name. What distinguishes a cathedral from a parish church is its special relationship with the bishop as the chief pastor of the diocese. The chair is the chair of the teacher rather than the throne of the ruler. The bishop is overseer and shepherd of the clergy and laity who minister word and sacraments and pastoral care in the parishes. The bishop's *cathedra* in the cathedral has its counterpart in every parish church – a special chair in the sanctuary for the bishop's use.

This cathedral is neither museum nor mausoleum, nor yet a decaying monument of an outworn faith. It continues to be what it always was, a vibrant centre through more than seven centuries in which God is acknowledged as man's creator, redeemer and sanctifier; where worship is offered every day in the Christian tradition from the rich treasury of church music that spans the centuries from the medieval plainsong to the new settings of contemporary composers. By no means the least reason why Christianity requires to be taken seriously and joyfully is its inherent capacity in every age to evoke from artists and musicians offerings of fresh response.

A cathedral, then, is a kind of monastery in which worship, song and prayer are offered every day. A cathedral is also a kind of theatre in which the Christian story is continually being presented in the eucharistic drama; 'in the round', as it were, with everyone participating – congregation, choir and clergy. A cathedral in these days is also a place much visited by pilgrims and tourists from all parts of the world, drawn to it by an attraction that many of those who come would find hard to explain. Perhaps there is a sleeping pilgrim who waits to be awakened in every tourist.

With this brief reflection on the original conception and continuing tradition of the building we can attend more relevantly to the structure itself. From end to end Salisbury is built in one style, a style that came to be called 'Early English' in spite of the fact that the style originated in the fertile Île de France, in the royal abbey of St Denis (consecrated in 1144). The style consists essentially of an ensemble of pointed arch and vault ribbed with thin webs of cut stone. What strikes us as design was in origin an engineering discovery which opened up a whole new architecture of variety and adventure. Whereas the whole weight of the old barrel vaults had to be carried by thick walls, the discovery of the pointed arch and the weight-bearing ribs enabled thrust to be focused on certain points rather than along the full run of wall. Weight-bearing pillars inside and buttresses outside made it possible to pierce the walls between the buttresses, to enlarge the windows, at first into tall thin lancets as in

Salisbury and later into vast areas of glass as in King's College Chapel at Cambridge. Technology became the servant of artistry. The development of coloured and painted glass in the twelfth and thirteenth centuries was one consequence of the larger apertures; another was new styles of tracery – such as can be seen in the Chapter House windows of a slightly later date than the cathedral lancets. The full glory of this gothic marriage of engineering and craftsman's art can be seen best at Chartres or Bourges or nearer home at Canterbury, whose choir was rebuilt in this style after the fire of 1174. Here the French influence is unmistakable; the account by the monk Gervase of the building of the choir of Canterbury makes clear that the builders were aware that they were using an invention that had been developed 'over the water'.

Unhappily Salisbury has been robbed of the medieval glass that filled the apertures of the nave and choir. Something of what we have lost can be imagined from two windows made up of fragments and to be seen towards the west end of the south nave aisle wall. The similarity in tone and feeling with glass of the thirteenth century in Canterbury and Chartres is immediately identifiable. In the three lancets of the great west window, a local Salisbury glazier, John Beare, assembled between 1819 and 1824 the variety of stained glass we now see. Some portions were already in the cathedral's possession: some were purchased in London, having been collected in France. The shields along the bottom had been removed from the Chapter House: these date from 1280. From left to right they read: a. Gilbert de Clare, Earl of Gloucester (1262–95); b. Not known; c. Eleanor of Provence, wife of Henry III (d. 1290); d. Louis IX of France, brother-in-law of Eleanor (1226–70); e. Henry III (1216–72); f. Richard, Earl of Cornwall, brother of Henry III (1225–72); g. Roger Bigod, Earl of Norfolk and Earl Marshal (1226–70).

Other medieval glass that survived the removal and destruction of all coloured glass by James Wyatt two hundred years ago is the thirteenth-century grisaille in the south window of the south-east transept. These fragments were found in the glazier's room above the vault of the Trinity Chapel and were put together in 1896. Celia Fiennes, who visited Salisbury between 1682 and 1696, wrote in her diary that 'the windows of the church, but specifically of the Quire, are very finely painted and largely of the history of the Bible'.

OPPOSITE: *The High Altar, with Prisoners of Conscience window and Moses window beyond, viewed through the choir stalls.*

LEFT: *Fragments of the oldest glass that has survived: the left lancet contains remains of a Jesse window (c. 1240), the right thirteenth-century fragments from the Chapter House and elsewhere.* RIGHT: *John Beare's collage in the three lancets of the west window.*

Detail from Prisoners of Conscience window.

In 1979 the dean and chapter invited M. Gabriel Loire from Chartres to design and make a modern window of glass in antique method for the five lancets of the Trinity Chapel. From the west end he has provided a mosaic of strong colour which catches the eye of the visitor and counteracts the otherwise grey, cool impression which so many people have found, as they say, 'disappointing'. As you move eastwards towards the window the symbols begin to define themselves; but only by sitting in front of the glass in the Trinity Chapel itself (ideally with a copy of the booklet describing the symbols) does the full meaning of the whole reveal itself to the observer. The theme of the window is 'Prisoners of Conscience'. In the three central lancets Christ is presented as a prisoner of conscience of the first century: he stands for truth against the lie, as do prisoners of conscience of all the centuries since, and especially of this twentieth century: these men and women 'valiant for truth' are represented by the faces in the two outside lancets. Wholly within the tradition and technique of the glassmakers of the century in which the cathedral was

built, Gabriel Loire's window is nonetheless original and contemporary
in style and in message. Words written by Wilfred Owen during the First
World War still apply:

> The scribes on all the people shove
> And brawl allegiance to the state,
> But they who love the greater love
> Lay down their life: they do not hate.

What makes the east window all the more important for the presenta-
tion of the building and of the Gospel is the long, uninterrupted vista
created by the removal of any screen between the nave and the area of the
choir and sanctuary. During the Middle Ages there was a stone screen or
pulpitum enclosing the choir area and creating in effect two churches as in
Wells or Winchester, Westminster Abbey or Canterbury. The medieval
pilgrim was not intended to see the vista presented to the visitor today. By
the end of the Middle Ages he would have been confronted by several
screens, high reredoses, elaborate chantries, parcloses and tombs of
astonishing richness.

What remains of the medieval *pulpitum* is to be seen against the west
wall of the Morning Chapel in the north-east transept. Very impressive it
must have been in its day, as the carvings of the foliage on the shafts that

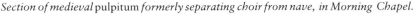

Section of medieval pulpitum *formerly separating choir from nave, in Morning Chapel.*

flank the niches still indicate. The middle niche on the right-hand side has recently been cleaned of overpainting and enough of the original medieval colouring is now exposed to give some idea of the splendour that confronted anyone coming into the nave. In its original position the niches held statues of English kings. This *pulpitum*, together with the magnificent organ by Renatus Harris, placed upon it in 1710, was removed by Wyatt at the end of the eighteenth century. In its place a new choir screen of stone was erected and upon it a new organ by Samuel Green. Wyatt's screen in its turn was removed when Sir Gilbert Scott was architect between 1860 and 1878. The entire choir area was redesigned: the stalls are made up of work of different periods; an elaborate marble reredos was placed behind the High Altar and a painted Skidmore metal choir screen marked off choir from nave. This screen, together with the reredos and much of Scott's furnishings, were themselves removed in the 1960s.

The coolness of the grey stone from the quarries at Chilmark is a little modified by the warmer tints of the Purbeck stone which provides the pillars in nave and transepts. The pillars of stone carry the weight; the darker shafts of Purbeck marble with their myriad imprisoned small fossils are decorative. Specially to be noticed is the graceful delicacy of the slender marble pillars that support the vaults of the Trinity Chapel. Francis Price who wrote a monograph on the cathedral in 1753 – from the point of view of a practical builder – expressed himself 'amazed at the vast boldness of the architect, who certainly piqued himself on leaving to posterity an instance of such small pillars bearing so great a load. One would not suppose them to stand so firm of themselves as even to resist the force of an ordinary wind.'

The colouring of the mouldings of the vaults of the Trinity Chapel was Scott's effort to recapture something of the medieval effect. What medieval vault painting was really like can best be seen in the recently preserved designs on the vault of the entrance to the Chapter House. Traces of medieval colour can be seen along the mouldings of vault ribs in the cathedral itself on sunny days.

The over-paintings on the vault of the high choir were done by Clayton and Bell on Scott's instructions. According to Celia Fiennes: 'The top of the quire is exactly painted and it looks as fresh as if new done though of 300 years standing.' That was her observation made about the year 1695.

OPPOSITE: *Interplay of arches in the choir transepts, with a glimpse of the roundels.*

Daniel Defoe in 1748 spoke of 'Paltry old painting in and over the choir'. Between these two observers and Scott had come the work of Wyatt who had 'buff-washed' the originals, as can be seen by observing the evidences of similar roundels on the vaults of the eastern transepts.

One conclusion can be drawn from Scott's repainted roundels. The High Altar must at one time have stood several yards to the west of its present position. The medallion of Christ in glory surrounded by roundels of the four evangelists must indicate by their position the fact that the altar was immediately below. This conclusion is further supported by the small windlass close to the pier on the north side of the presbytery. This windlass was most probably used to raise and lower a veil to cover the altar reredos during Lent. East of the Christ medallion in the vault are twelve symbols which serve to remind us of the medieval capacity to see life whole and see it one: the symbols typify the twelve months of the year: January, warming at a fire; February, drinking wine; March, delving; April, sowing; May, hawking; June, flowers; July, reaping; August, threshing; September, fruit; October, brewing; November, cutting wood; December, killing the fatted pig.

Such evidence as there is indicates the centre of the Trinity Chapel as the site of the shrine of St Osmund, who was canonised by decree of Pope Callixtus in 1456, a long time from his death at Old Sarum in 1099; a gap which illustrates the vagaries of the canonisation process. We have no description of the shrine. What we do know is that the commissioners of Henry VIII in 1539 removed gold and jewels. Two men worked for nine days to take to pieces the shrine itself; further demolition followed later in the year. From this we must infer that it was an elaborate structure.

From the Chapter Act Book for 15 February 1472/3 we learn that 'the work of the new silver shrine of St Osmund commenced this present year in costly manner (sumptuose)'. Letters had been sent to 38 persons, sealed with the seal of the chapter saying:

The saint's precious reliques deserve to be set not in a poor chest, but rather, as is the case in some other churches, in gold and precious stones. We have laid foundations in marble and have raised a notable structure and have begun to make a silver shrine. At the present time when we had hoped to see the work half-completed we are, sad to say, forced to desist from the undertaking all of a sudden through want of money. To tell the truth we have contributed as much as we were able from our own resources, the Common Treasury is exhausted: the devotion which our people showed of old has become cold . . . we therefore earnestly beg you, my very dear brother . . . that your hand be opened as wide as possible with the utmost liberality . . .

One of the Old Testament bas-reliefs (of Adam and Eve) in the Chapter House.

It is generally thought that the almost black stone coffin lid on the plinth at the south-west corner of the Trinity Chapel with the carved inscription ANNO MXCIX (the date of St Osmund's death) and the table-topped monument between pillars on the south nave arcade, with three openings in each side (to enable sick people and pilgrims to place arms or legs through the holes in the hope of a cure from the presence of the saint's bones), were both included in the structure of the shrine. More problematical is the marble slab with relief effigy of a bishop and a verse in Latin round the edge of the slab, near the west end of the nave on the south side. Variously attributed by antiquaries to Bishop Jocelin and Bishop Roger, there are those now who argue that it belonged to the grave of Bishop Osmund at Old Sarum but was carved at a later date than his original burial. Each of these associated stones has been moved in the course of time, making it difficult even for the most skilled of scholarly detectives to reconstruct the whole story with complete confidence.

As a visitor wanders slowly round and allows his or her eye to take in the small as well as the large, all kinds of decorative carvings will be seen on tombs, on capitals of pillars, at the springing points of vault ribs, on bosses at the high points of intersection of ribs. The masons enjoyed themselves. Their enjoyment can be guessed also from the many carved faces that bequeath to us a medieval portrait gallery of unnamed contemporaries. An especially fine circlet of such stone portraits can be seen in the Chapter House above the canons' stalls that are carved out of the walls. Above these stalls is another of Salisbury's treasures – sculptured episodes from the books of Genesis and Exodus.

Visitors to the cathedral are much attracted by the new embroideries, the work of the Sarum Guild of Embroiderers formed in 1978 from students of a class working under the guidance of Jane Lemon. Examples of their work are to be seen in the Baptistry in the Morning Chapel, in the adjacent Audley Chantry, in the Chapel of St Lawrence in the south transept, and most powerfully in the 'Energy' frontal when that is in place at the High Altar. In this frontal the energies of the galactic universe, of the biological universe and of the dimension of divine grace are related. The colours reflect the colours of the east window: the symbols of the crown of thorns and the chalice are also to be seen in that window. The chalice is shaped from a small thirteenth-century chalice found in the tomb of William Longespée and to be seen in the case of medieval silver in the Chapter House. In addition new vestments and copes have revived something of the colour and drama that enhance the movement of the liturgy.

From the contents we come back to the container. Here on the inside we can see how nave, choir and transepts have been strengthened to sustain the tonnage of tower and spire that presses on the four main pillars at the crossing. The slight but definite bending of these main pillars can be seen by standing beneath each one in turn. The pillars of transepts and choir lean outwards away from the crossing. The strainer arches between the transepts and the crossing hold the main pillars steady in an east-west direction. A similar support in the shape of inverted arches (reminiscent of those under the tower at Wells) hold the tall pillars of the arches of the two eastern transepts. Standing beneath the tower at the main crossing the observer can see slanting buttresses introduced in all directions at

*The focal centre of cathedral worship: cross and candlesticks carved by Head Carpenter in
1982; the 'Energy' frontal designed and made by the Sarum Guild of Embroiderers.*

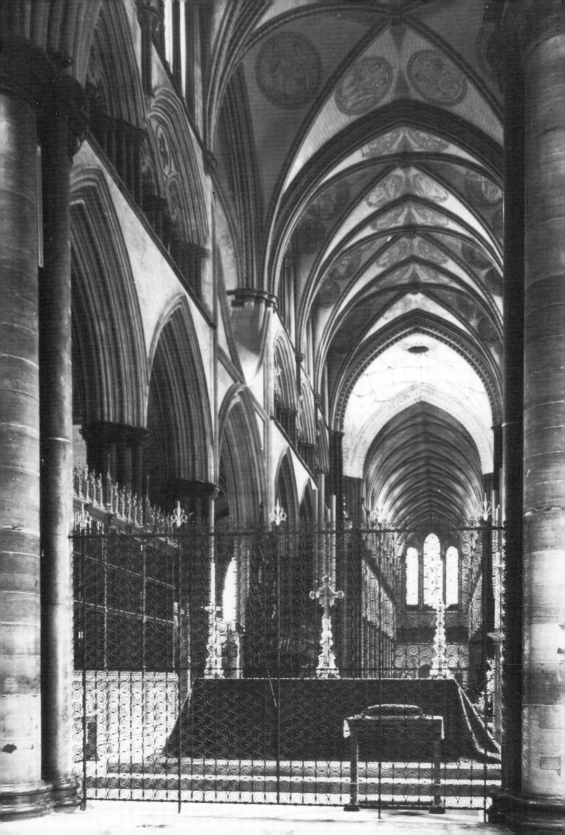

triforium and clerestory level taking thrust off the main pillars and distributing it into nave, choir and transepts on both sides.

But what of the higher reaches of the tower itself? It was Bishop Seth Ward (1667–89), distinguished mathematician and one of the founder members of the Royal Society, who called in his friend Sir Christopher Wren to survey the condition of the tower and spire. In his report of 1668 Wren commends the 'many large bandes of iron within and without (the tower) keyed together with much industry and exactnesse . . . without which the spire would spread open the walls of the tower nor would it stand one minute'. He was so impressed by the fineness of the Salisbury ironwork that, in spite of his normal distrust of the method, he decided to use iron again: 'because the artist at first hath much trusted in Iron, I should advise its further use in the spire'. He then describes the making of iron chains of eight 'links' to encircle the spire within and without and adds '*note*, these irons will be best wrought at some Port Towne where they worke Anchors and other large work for shipps for I have found by experience that large worke cannot be wrought sounde with little fires and small bellows'. The tradition of iron banding was continued two hundred years later by Scott. On two occasions, in 1560 and in 1741, the spire was struck by lightning, but the craftsmanship of the medieval builders in arranging the distribution of thrust, coupled with the expert strengthening of the tower itself with interior cross bands by architects and structural engineers in the centuries since, has enabled the tallest spire in England to stand steady in all winds and weathers.

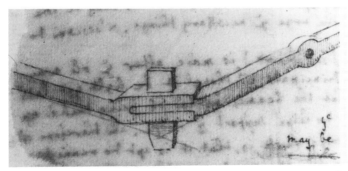

Illustration from Sir Christopher Wren's notebook (1668): ironwork for strengthening the tower.

OPPOSITE: *Looking west from the Trinity Chapel down the full length of the cathedral.*

...DIE ARE TO STERVE.

ELLEONORA IACET CONIVX MEA CHARA SVB ISTO
MARMORE. NI CHARAM FLEVERO, MARMOR ERO
FÆMINA MVLTIPLICI VIRTVTIS AMORE DECORA
ILLECEBRASQ SOLI SPREVIT, AMORE POLI
SANCTA FVIT, SANCTE VIXIT SANCTEQ RECESSIT
IN CÆLO TANDEM SANCTIOR ILLA MANET.

T:S: MARITVS DEFLEVIT

4 The Use of Sarum

The Use of Sarum is an expression that covers the arrangements made for the ordering of Divine Worship in Salisbury Cathedral during the Middle Ages and to be found in the original manuscripts and more recent publications by liturgists who have studied the medieval service books. The forms of worship evolved at Old Sarum and transferred to New Sarum were complicated and could have become chaotic in practice had there been no agreement about the words to be said or sung and the movements to be made. These regulations were detailed. The manuscripts that contain them are to be found in various libraries. But as a result of careful study of these manuscripts by liturgical scholars we know how worship was conducted in medieval times in both the first and second of the cathedrals at Salisbury.

The book that controlled what should be done and by whom was called the Consuetudinary: it contained a code of customs and is the principal authority for what came to be known as the Use of Sarum. The conclusion of scholars points to Richard Poore as the compiler of this document, incorporating earlier regulations drawn up by Bishop Osmund. The probable date of the earliest extant manuscript is 1210, suggesting that it was the last work of Richard Poore as Dean at Old Sarum (1197–1215) rather than an early work of his as Bishop of New Sarum (1217–28). The Consuetudinary was concerned in particular to define the duties of persons in connection with the services of worship.

A second book, called the Customary, was a handbook of reference in rehearsing the usual services and was an abstract from the larger Consuetudinary which was the definitive authority in all things liturgical.

A third book, known as the Ordinal, was a service book for use in the choir. This book provided in detail for practical purposes the more general liturgical and ceremonial principles laid down in the Consuetudinary. It was the Ordinal which co-ordinated the uses of other service

OPPOSITE: *The tomb of Elihonor Sadler (d. 1622), wife of Thomas Sadler, Registrar of the diocese. They entertained James I at the 'King's House' in the Close, where they lived.*

A carved angel in the choir.

books – of which there were several. For the Mass there were five separate books – sacramentary, epistle book, gospel book, gradual and troper. For the choir offices there were the collectar, legend, hymnal and antiphoner. The provisions of the Ordinal make clear how the different parts of the service contained in the separate books were to be fitted together; instructions in red letters (rubrics) gave directions about the way things were to be done.

All such books were written by hand on parchment. In the course of time scribes became more skilled in getting more words into smaller spaces until complete books could incorporate what previously had required separate volumes. A missal could hold together all that was needed for the celebration of the Eucharist. A breviary could hold together all that was needed for the choir offices, that is for the hours of prayer offered in choir; the night office of Mattins was followed by the seven day hours of Lauds, Prime, Terce, Sext, Nones, Vespers and Compline. This arrangement of the Offices had been fixed in detail in the sixth century by St Benedict in his Rule for monks and monasteries. He called it the Work of God – Opus Dei. Each 'hour' consisted of psalms, hymns, Bible readings, antiphons, versicles and responses and prayers. Briefly, the round of worship in the secular cathedrals staffed by canons was the same as that in monasteries staffed by monks; a pattern that had been developed over many centuries in monastic communities.

The books that carried the musical notations for the services of worship were very large indeed, in order that two or more cantors standing at a tall lectern could read the notes in the flickering light cast by candles. In the course of time the invention of printing made possible further reduction in the size and weight of all service books while increasing the content that could be bound within covers.

During the twelfth and thirteenth centuries there was a considerable borrowing from the Sarum books by the chapters of other cathedrals. It was the texts of the Sarum rites which were chiefly used by the compilers of the first Book of Common Prayer in English in 1549. In addition to the words and movements of worship a variety of ceremonies developed, such as the veiling of crosses on altars during Lent, and the provision of processions before the main Mass on Sundays and Festivals, on Wednesdays and Fridays during Lent for the singing of the Litany; also on Rogation days before Ascension Day for intercessions for seedtime and harvest. Other processions were arranged exceptionally in times of national emergency – drought, plague or war. The naves of cathedrals provided an ideal setting for processions and pageantry, being without seats except for a low stone bench along the walls of the aisles. No doubt something of the symbolism of life as a journey and the custom of pilgrimage was embedded in this custom of processions through the building and outside. The dramatic element in medieval worship was prominent. Many of these medieval ceremonies, especially those relating to Holy Week and Easter (suppressed during the period of the Reformation) have been revived in revised form in most cathedrals during the past century and a half.

For the parish congregation the most striking change from the medieval to the Tudor, Elizabethan and later periods must have been the change from the Latin language to the English: the simplification in the number of the services and their content further marked the change in cathedrals. The seven 'Hours' of prayer were reduced to two – the now familiar Morning and Evening Prayer of the Book of Common Prayer of 1662. Not everything was changed: many canticles and prayers continued, but in translation. All the psalms in the translation of Miles Coverdale were

arranged to be said or sung every month. Readings from the Old and New Testaments were much longer than the brief extracts used in the medieval Offices. The intentions of the reformers of the liturgy are memorably set out in the Prefaces to the Prayer Book of 1662. One quotation is relevant here: 'And whereas heretofore there hath been great diversity in saying and singing in Churches within this Realm; some following Salisbury use, some Hereford use, and some the use of Bangor, some of York, some of Lincoln; now from henceforth all the whole Realm shall have but one use.'

An interesting Salisbury example of the process of change during this long period of unrest and reform can be seen in a fifteenth-century manuscript 'Processionale' in the Cathedral Library. At the top of one of the inserted leaves in the manuscript near the end of the volume is a memorandum (in the handwriting of an Elizabethan chapter clerk) relating to the history of the manuscript itself. It reads in translation:

On the seventeenth of October AD 1573 John Pers (Dean), Richard Chandler, Thomas Lancaster, James Proctor, John Coleshill and John Bolde, residentiary canons of the Cathedral Church of Salisbury meeting officially in the Chapter House of the said Church to do Chapter business, inspected this book and found many superstitious items in it contrary to the Word of God and the laws of this realm of England.

Wherefore being moved by reverence to God and obedience towards the Prince we unanimously decreed that whatever in this book was not in accordance with Holy Scripture and was contrary to the laws of this realm of England should be utterly obliterated, and we ordered such to be obliterated in these writings.

The decree was signed by all those present and witnessed by Wil. Blacker, public notary and chapter clerk. The manuscript shows that a pen was drawn across several pages in the volume. The list of relicts had at an earlier date been vigorously blacked out with inquisitor's black ink: references to the Pope and to St Thomas of Canterbury were erased.

The essential use of the cathedral today is the same as it has always been – to acknowledge the reality, the revelation and the claims of God as made known in Jesus Christ as paradigm of the mystery and meaning of being alive and being human. This affirmation is the *raison d'être* of the cathedral building itself; this was the motivation and faith of its builders. A cathedral is both a protest and a proclamation – a protest against all

OPPOSITE: *The High Altar seen through arcade of tomb of Bishop (1854–69) Walter Hamilton, with arcade beyond of tomb of Bishop (1229–46) Robert Bingham.*

ideologies and political systems which deny or diminish the spirituality, dignity and true liberty of human persons, and a proclamation of the Christian Way as an invitation to pilgrimage, an offered route by which human beings can find help in their search for the answer to their fundamental questions: 'Who am I?' 'What may I hope?' 'What should I do?'

Within the contemporary life of the cathedral community, this affirmation is made daily in acts of worship (a word that means 'to honour and adore'). The texts used for these offerings are contained partly in the Book of Common Prayer of 1662 and partly in the Alternative Service Book of 1980. Each day the two 'Hours' into which the medieval offices were conflated by the reformers, Morning Prayer and Evening Prayer (sometimes called Mattins and Evensong) are offered either by saying or by singing. Evensong is normally sung each day by the cathedral choir or by a visiting choir in their absence. Mattins is said daily and sung on Sundays. Every morning the Eucharist is offered in one or other of the chapels and on Sunday is sung at 10 a.m. and sometimes sung

Sarum Ordinal: fourteenth century.

in the evening on Greater Saints' Days. A sermon is preached at both the Eucharist and Mattins on Sundays. In addition to this regular round of prayer, penitence and praise there are special occasions such as ordinations, baptisms, confirmations, thanksgiving-memorials, weddings, school services, carol services before Christmas, a traditional procession on Palm Sunday and on the evening of Advent Sunday. During this Advent Procession, entitled 'From Darkness to Light', upwards of 800 candles are lit as choir and clergy move around the cathedral with pauses for readings of relevant passages from the Bible and the singing of antiphons and Advent hymns. The dramatic effect of the move from total darkness to the warm glow of the living flames of many candles has to be experienced to be understood. It symbolises the story of the long march and long search of everyman, both the history and the hope.

Cathedral worship without the enrichment of choral and organ music is virtually unthinkable. What is perhaps not widely known is the amount of music that has been written for use in worship. The repertoire available for cathedral choirs stretches from the medieval plainsong to composers of today. In the Salisbury repertoire there are twenty settings for the Eucharist, a hundred for the Canticles and many variants for Responses and Psalms. The reservoir of anthems reaches three hundred: these are choral songs in which passages from scripture and other literature are set to music to be sung at Mattins or Evensong or during the receiving of the sacrament at Holy Communion. The names of the musical contributors to this tradition shine like a galaxy of stars, beginning with the nameless composers of plainsong and continuing through the centuries in a variety of styles and interpretations.

The earliest reference to organs at Salisbury is in 1480 when there would seem to have been two, one in the choir and one in the body of the church. By 1539 the Great Organ stood over the entrance to the choir, above the stone *pulpitum*. Anticipating the Act of 1644 which ordered the demolition of all organs throughout England, the dean and chapter in 1643 'deemed it prudent in order to save the organ from destruction and in hope of better times to have it taken down and the material safely preserved'. At the Restoration of Charles II in 1660, when many cathedrals found themselves without music, organ or choir, Salisbury benefited from its foresight and in 1661 the organ was re-erected by Thomas Harris. The Renatus Harris organ of 1710 was the first in England with four manuals. In 1792 George III's gift of a new organ was placed over a new stone choir screen which replaced the medieval

South arcade of the nave, lit by afternoon sun.

Choristers in procession.

pulpitum. The builder was Samuel Green of Isleworth, who built over fifty organs in his lifetime – including twelve for cathedrals. This organ is now in the Church of St Thomas à Becket in Salisbury. Finally, the present organ, built by Henry Willis in 1876 and the gift of Miss Chafyn Grove, was placed on both sides of the choir. A list of the names of organists is painted on the organ case in the south choir aisle.

The chanter (now called precentor) rules the choir 'in respect of raising or lowering the pitch of chants'. To the precentor also belongs the 'instruction and discipline of the boys as well as their admission and ordering in the quire'. The third of the Bishop Osmund's 'Principal Persons' was and is the *archischola* or chancellor, who had responsibility in 'ruling schools and as corrector of the books'. Bishop Osmund established at Old Sarum both a song school and a grammar school.

The choristers have been housed in the Close in various places at different periods – in the Hungerford Chantry (no. 54), in no. 5 and in Braybrooke's Canonry (no. 58) until they moved into the schoolhouse known as Wren Hall built in 1714. The move from Wren Hall to the bishop's palace took place in 1947 when Bishop Lovett finally left the ancient episcopal residence. Since then choristers have ceased to be separately housed; they are for educational purposes boarders in Salisbury Cathedral School and are extracted from there for their singing practices. The 'crocodile' of small cloaked figures is a special feature of the life of the Close. For 700 years they practised their singing in the long room behind no. 5, adjoining the residence of the organist. Since 1970 choir practices take place in the former muniment room above the Canons' Vestry. The present Cathedral School of 130 boys continues to be governed by the dean and chapter in the medieval tradition.

Salisbury Cathedral choir today consists of sixteen trebles, two altos, two tenors, two basses. It goes several times a year to sing in various parish churches of the diocese and the cathedral organists give help and encouragement to the organists in the parishes. Every year there is a Diocesan Music Festival in the cathedral, as well as in Wimborne Minster and Sherborne Abbey. The cost of maintaining the music of the cathedral is upwards of £50,000 per annum, a figure that does not include any major work needing to be done from time to time on the organ itself.

Every July for the past twenty-five years the three cathedral choirs of Chichester, Winchester and Salisbury have combined, under the direction of their organists, to present in each of these cathedrals in rotation the Southern Cathedrals' Festival. The Festival is essentially a celebration of the liturgy of the three days; with two evening concerts and a late-night fringe event in addition. A new piece of choral music is often commissioned for the Festival. Other occasional events involving the choir are annual broadcasts of Evensong on Radio 3, television presentations from time to time, and a share when required in concerts given in the cathedral by the Salisbury Musical Society.

In a treasured passage in his life of the poet-priest, George Herbert of Bemerton, Izaak Walton wrote:

His chiefest recreation was Music, in which heavenly Art he was a most excellent Master, and did himself compose many divine Hymns and Anthems, which he set and sung to his Lute or Viol: And though he was a lover of retiredness, yet his love of Music was such, that he went usually twice every week on certain appointed days, to the Cathedral Church in Salisbury; and at his return would say, That his time spent in Prayer and Cathedral Music, elevated his Soul, and was his Heaven upon Earth. But before his return thence to Bemerton he would usually sing and play his part at an appointed private Music-meeting; and, to justify this practice, he would often say, Religion does not banish mirth, but only moderates and sets rules to it.

The continuity of the cathedral as a community through centuries of

Library, Chapter House and Cathedral School grounds.

change can be measured not only by the continuity of the building and the worship with its musical accompaniment, but by the existence of muniments and manuscripts and books. The muniments or archives are considerable in quantity and variety. There are the records of the decisions of the dean and chapter; there are seals, leases, indulgences, accounts and correspondence. It is in these documents essentially that the life-story of the cathedral is embedded and can only be extracted with scholarly patience, and for early centuries the student requires a command of medieval Latin and a skill in deciphering calligraphy.

The building which contains the Library can be seen above the north end of the eastern vault of the cloisters. When built in 1446 it covered the whole length of this cloister walk. The southern half housed the manuscripts and books: the northern half formed a lecture room where successive chancellors expounded the mysteries of theology. In 1758 the southern half of this building was taken down 'the whole being found much too heavy to be properly supported by the Cloysters'. The walls of the northern half were lowered and covered with a lighter roof. This section now contains the inherited Library.

Among the contents are over 180 manuscripts dating from the ninth to the fifteenth centuries. Of these, fifty-three, written between 1089–1125, have been judged by the distinguished palaeographer, the late Neil Ker, to have been written at Old Sarum either during the lifetime of Bishop Osmund or soon after his death.

In the centuries since, many gifts of books have enriched the original collection. There are some forty incunabula. A very valuable collection of contemporary pamphlets of the period of the Protestant reformation was given by Bishop Edmund Gheast, one of the revisers of the Elizabethan prayer book. He was Bishop of Salisbury from 1571–77. His memorial brass may be seen in the floor of the Morning Chapel. The most valuable from the seventeenth century was that of Bishop Seth Ward who died in 1689. A founder member of the Royal Society, Ward's books indicate the breadth of his scholarly interests. The eighteenth century was a dismal period of neglect brightened only by the gift by Canon Isaac Walton of over one hundred volumes, of which twenty-nine belonged to his more famous father, Izaak Walton. Further generous gifts were received during the nineteenth and twentieth centuries.

The new bookcases in the Library.

Essentially the cathedral library is a private library of manuscripts and rare books to be studied by scholars. From 1978 until July 1983 it was closed for complete restoration. New bookshelves designed by Alan Rome, the cathedral architect, and made by cathedral carpenters from the wood of elm trees that until recently stood in the Close, now provide a home worthy of the books and of the scribes and scholars who wrote them and of the benefactors who gave them.

The most noticeable recent change in the Use of Sarum (to continue the wider application of the word 'use') is not a change initiated by the dean and chapter but by the worldwide spread of tourism. More and more people are discovering cathedrals. Individuals have for centuries made journeys to see cathedrals; for many years scholars and artists have made cathedrals more accessible through books and paintings: there must be many thousands whose first encounter with Salisbury was the sight of a painting of the cathedral by John Constable or William Turner. Deans and chapters, roused from Barchester slumbers, found themselves compelled to attend to the presence of the hundreds of thousands who poured into their cathedrals, uninvited but not unwelcome, and to interpret for them the significance of the building they had come to see. At Salisbury we have a splendid team of voluntary guides to speak with small groups about the building and the community; every day a team of men and women from one of the parishes in the diocese attends to the needs of visitors in the refectory; the bookshop is staffed by voluntary helpers. All in all, including ladies who arrange flowers, servers who assist at times of worship, embroiderers, stewards and the groups already mentioned, there are some 400 men and women who give time in one way and another to serve the cathedral and those who come to it. The kind of numbers visiting cathedrals can best be indicated by the following round figures for 1982:

St Paul's, Canterbury and York	2,000,000 +
Durham, Coventry, Salisbury	500,000 +
Wells	350,000 +
Worcester	150,000 +

Inevitably arrangements to accommodate such large numbers cost money and call for more paid staff in addition to the voluntary helpers. Wear and tear is increased as well as dust and litter. Various persuasions have been adopted to encourage visitors to contribute to the upkeep of the cathedrals they have chosen to visit. Some cathedrals, of which Salisbury was the first, arrange entrance to the building through one door so that they are able to request a voluntary contribution of an amount suggested – well below the charge levied at the great houses, but considerably above the average gift which hitherto the average visitor had thought appropriate. At Salisbury all money received from visitors on entry is placed in a preservation fund to be used solely for the maintenance work on the building itself; the repair of roofs, parapets, pinnacles and buttresses, together with continuing professional monitoring of any movement of the masonry of tower and spire and the strengthening of existing supports.

In requesting a voluntary contribution of a suggested sum the dean and chapter have always in mind their double responsibility – for a living Church, its spiritual integrity and Christian mission; and for an ancient building which is an architectural treasure of the national heritage. With no financial support from government sources the dean and chapter have to raise the money for the maintenance of the latter. It seemed only right and proper that those members of the world public who wished to enjoy the heritage should be asked to contribute to the upkeep of the fabric. The system of controlled entrance, therefore, is geared to the summer tourist influx. On each weekday from Easter until the end of October, from 10 a.m. – 5 p.m., the system is in operation. These times avoid any overlap with times of public worship; a request to enter without payment for personal prayer is accepted, with an invitation to make a contribution in one of the boxes inside the cathedral. Almost all visitors make the contribution asked for, often adding to the amount suggested. But it has to be admitted that the prayerfulness of the cathedral during the day is greatly diminished by the background of noise caused by hundreds of feet on stone floors and the more than murmur of voices. However, those who knew the cathedral in the days before the system was introduced have said that the general behaviour of visitors has noticeably improved. At every hour one of the priests from the diocese, acting as chaplain for the day, invites whoever is in the cathedral to stand where they are or to sit down for a brief recollection, intercession and concluding Lord's Prayer – each speaking in his or her own language. The response to this request is impressive.

In medieval times the nave of a cathedral, that is the large area west of the choir, empty of pews and chairs, was regarded as reserved for the people of the city. Local citizens used this area for a variety of purposes. It was a kind of public square where they could meet and talk. Municipal and business affairs were debated in the nave. The nave of Salisbury in our time is also a gathering-place for events other than services of worship. In recent years large audiences have come to hear great orchestras, with distinguished conductors and soloists. The availability of a large auditorium has made it possible for the organisers of the Salisbury Festival each September to engage musical ensembles of large size and excellent calibre.

Last but not least in value in the present use of the cathedral is its employment as an educational visual aid. A skilled and imaginative teacher can use the cathedral to introduce a group of schoolchildren to a wide variety of subjects – architectural history and design, embroidery, music, sculpture, woodcarving, stained glass, heraldry, national history and biography with the aid of effigies on tombs and inscriptions on wall memorials, together with the art symbols of the Christian story, liturgical places and their meaning, the biblical literature, the story of the spread of Christianity and the beliefs of the Christian community. The dean and chapter have prepared two audio-visual tapes to be shown in school in advance of a visit to increase awareness and recognition, as well as brochures to enable children to discover things in the cathedral for themselves. It is good to see young men and women from local art schools making drawings of the building and its decorative embellishments. The workshops train and employ apprentices in stonework, carpentry, glazing and plumbing.

> And, gazing at the forms there flung
> Against the sky by one unsung . . .
>
> Muse that some minds so modest be
> As to renounce fame's fairest fee,
>
> (Like him who crystallized on this spot
> His visionings, but lies forgot,
>
> And many a medieval one
> Whose symmetries salute the sun)
>
> While others boom a baseless claim,
> And upon nothing rear a name.

THOMAS HARDY *The Abbey Mason*

A Checklist of Dates

1668	Bishop Seth Ward calls in Christopher Wren to survey the fabric: strengthening of tower by iron bondings.
1667–89	Bishop Seth Ward refurnishes the choir.
1738	Timbers within spire substantially repaired.
1741	Tower struck by lightning: smouldering fire broke into flame on following day among timber braces of spire, but quickly extinguished.
1757	Octagonal third storey of freestanding bell-tower ordered to be removed: work done 1777.
1758	Southern half of fifteenth-century library demolished.
1781	Moses window inserted at high east end of choir.
1789	James Wyatt appointed architect: chaotic state of churchyard repaired.
1790 onwards	Bell-tower demolished; also Beauchamp and Hungerford Chantry chapels; stonework from Chantry Chapels placed in Trinity Chapel; 'High Altar' placed at east wall of Trinity Chapel; screens removed from chapels in transepts; thirteenth-century *pulpitum* and organ by Renatus Harris (1710) removed from entrance to choir; *pulpitum* partially re-erected on west wall of north-east transept; new stone screen surmounted by organ by Samuel Green (gift of George III) placed at entrance to choir; new bishop's throne, pulpit and canopies for choir stalls; all remaining medieval glass removed and most of it deposited in town ditch; many tombs removed from original positions and set between pillars of the nave arcades; resurrection window of painted glass by Sir Joshua Reynolds placed in central lancet at east end.
1854	Reynolds's window removed. Restoration of Chapter House: some replacing of broken heads of sculptures in spandrils of arcade: central pillar rebuilt with new capital and base.
1860–78	Sir Gilbert Scott appointed architect; removed Wyatt's furnishings and fittings in choir and Trinity Chapel; introduced encaustic tiles in floor of choir; new bishop's throne, marble reredos and painted metal choir screen by Skidmore: Scott introduced (following Wren's earlier work) an arrangement of diagonal iron bars from corner to corner of tower connected with bars encircling external buttresses at base of the Early English tower. Restoration of west front; remaining eight medieval statues restored: Redfern added 50 new figures by 1869 and ten more later – an outstanding achievement.
1905–10	Underpinning of west front.
1913	New canopies for choir stalls by C. E. Ponting.
1937	Turret staircases of tower and corner windows built up to give extra strength.

Elisabeth Frink's Madonna *with friends.*

1949–51	Top 30 feet of spire rebuilt.
1950–60	Much of Scott's work in choir, including marble reredos, removed; filigree metal screen added behind High Altar; new communion rails and furniture; new pulpit of wood by Randoll Blacking and episcopal coats of arms and names of medieval prebends added to choir stalls; floor tiles replaced with squares of polished Purbeck marble; move to replace Clutton's grisaille windows in Chapter House with plain glass thwarted by public outcry; Skidmore's metal choir screen removed.
1967–69	Reinforcing of top of tower.
1978–83	Restoration of the Library.
1979	Sarum Guild of Embroiderers formed.
1980	Unveiling by Yehudi Menuhin of *Prisoners of Conscience* window, designed and made by M. Gabriel Loire of Chartres.
1982	Elisabeth Frink's *Walking Madonna* placed outside north porch.